THE CASTRO REGIME'S ONGOING VIOLATIONS OF CIVIL AND POLITICAL RIGHTS

HEARING

BEFORE THE

SUBCOMMITTEE ON AFRICA, GLOBAL HEALTH, GLOBAL HUMAN RIGHTS, AND INTERNATIONAL ORGANIZATIONS

OF THE

COMMITTEE ON FOREIGN AFFAIRS

HOUSE OF REPRESENTATIVES

ONE HUNDRED FOURTEENTH CONGRESS

SECOND SESSION

JULY 13, 2016

Serial No. 114–219

Printed for the use of the Committee on Foreign Affairs

Available via the World Wide Web: http://www.foreignaffairs.house.gov/ or http://www.gpo.gov/fdsys/

U.S. GOVERNMENT PUBLISHING OFFICE

20–745PDF   WASHINGTON : 2016

For sale by the Superintendent of Documents, U.S. Government Publishing Office
Internet: bookstore.gpo.gov   Phone: toll free (866) 512–1800; DC area (202) 512–1800
Fax: (202) 512–2104   Mail: Stop IDCC, Washington, DC 20402–0001

COMMITTEE ON FOREIGN AFFAIRS

EDWARD R. ROYCE, California, *Chairman*

CHRISTOPHER H. SMITH, New Jersey
ILEANA ROS-LEHTINEN, Florida
DANA ROHRABACHER, California
STEVE CHABOT, Ohio
JOE WILSON, South Carolina
MICHAEL T. McCAUL, Texas
TED POE, Texas
MATT SALMON, Arizona
DARRELL E. ISSA, California
TOM MARINO, Pennsylvania
JEFF DUNCAN, South Carolina
MO BROOKS, Alabama
PAUL COOK, California
RANDY K. WEBER SR., Texas
SCOTT PERRY, Pennsylvania
RON DeSANTIS, Florida
MARK MEADOWS, North Carolina
TED S. YOHO, Florida
CURT CLAWSON, Florida
SCOTT DesJARLAIS, Tennessee
REID J. RIBBLE, Wisconsin
DAVID A. TROTT, Michigan
LEE M. ZELDIN, New York
DANIEL DONOVAN, New York

ELIOT L. ENGEL, New York
BRAD SHERMAN, California
GREGORY W. MEEKS, New York
ALBIO SIRES, New Jersey
GERALD E. CONNOLLY, Virginia
THEODORE E. DEUTCH, Florida
BRIAN HIGGINS, New York
KAREN BASS, California
WILLIAM KEATING, Massachusetts
DAVID CICILLINE, Rhode Island
ALAN GRAYSON, Florida
AMI BERA, California
ALAN S. LOWENTHAL, California
GRACE MENG, New York
LOIS FRANKEL, Florida
TULSI GABBARD, Hawaii
JOAQUIN CASTRO, Texas
ROBIN L. KELLY, Illinois
BRENDAN F. BOYLE, Pennsylvania

AMY PORTER, *Chief of Staff*   THOMAS SHEEHY, *Staff Director*
JASON STEINBAUM, *Democratic Staff Director*

————

SUBCOMMITTEE ON AFRICA, GLOBAL HEALTH, GLOBAL HUMAN RIGHTS, AND INTERNATIONAL ORGANIZATIONS

CHRISTOPHER H. SMITH, New Jersey, *Chairman*

MARK MEADOWS, North Carolina
CURT CLAWSON, Florida
SCOTT DesJARLAIS, Tennessee
DANIEL DONOVAN, New York

KAREN BASS, California
DAVID CICILLINE, Rhode Island
AMI BERA, California

CONTENTS

THE CASTRO REGIME'S ONGOING VIOLATIONS OF CIVIL AND POLITICAL RIGHTS

TUESDAY, JULY 13, 2016

House of Representatives,
Subcommittee on Africa, Global Health,
Global Human Rights, and International Organizations,
Committee on Foreign Affairs,
Washington, DC.

The subcommittee met, pursuant to notice, at 2 o'clock p.m., in room 2172 Rayburn House Office Building, Hon. Christopher H. Smith (chairman of the subcommittee) presiding.

Mr. SMITH. The subcommittee will come to order. And first let me begin by apologizing for the delay. There were a large series of votes in the House which precluded our meeting at the appointed time, so I do thank you for your forbearance.

Good afternoon. It has been 1 year and 8 months since President Obama announced a major change in our country's policy toward Cuba. It has been 11 months since Secretary Kerry visited Havana and reopened our Embassy, and it has been nearly 4 months since our President visited Cuba. Clearly, a lot has changed in just over 1½ years but for the people of Cuba, particularly those espousing fundamental human rights, what has changed?

Today we will examine the sorry state of the civil and political rights in the Castro brothers' Cuba, and how despite all the promises by the administration and that an opening to Cuba would lead to greater opening domestically for the Cuban people, we still see political repression, including it must be noted repression directed at the Afro-Cuban population. And in the past, this subcommittee has had a previous hearing where we focused in great part on that terrible repression.

This is not the first time this subcommittee has expressed concern about the lack of openness to democracy and the mistreatment of dissenters in Cuba. In fact, one of our witnesses, the courageous Dr. Oscar Biscet, offered dramatic testimony before this subcommittee in February 2012 when he testified via telephone from the U.S. Interests Section in Havana after evading the Cuban police to get there.

Likewise, on February 5, 2015, we held a hearing entitled "Human Rights in Cuba: An Opportunity Squandered," wherein we asked whether the Obama administration had used the considerable leverage that it wields to better the condition of the Cuban people, or whether it was squandering the opportunity.

Since then our fear that the administration has not been pushing sufficiently for the release of political prisoners and other human rights concerns has only grown with the focus on President Obama's legacy instead of on the Cuban people.

For example, when President Obama made his visit to Cuba, he and Raul Castro appeared in a photo opportunity press conference. CNN's Jim Acosta, much to his credit, asked the hard question about Cuba's political prisoners. Raul Castro, much to his discredit, denied that there were any political prisoners in Cuba. "Give me the list of the political prisoners and I will release them immediately," Castro taunted. "Just mention the list," he said. President Obama did not present him with a list.

Well, Mr. President, I have the list right here of 50 political prisoners compiled by our good friend and colleague, Ileana Ros-Lehtinen, and without objection we'll insert that list into the record and we will send it to the Embassy here in Washington for Cuba. And, hopefully, it will be then sent down to Raul Castro. This is the list that President Obama should have had in his breast pocket ready to pull out when Raul Castro dared him to call his bluff.

When I came to Congress in 1981 with Ronald Reagan, in the days of the old Soviet Union, one of the first issues I worked on was the plight of Soviet Jews and refuseniks who were imprisoned or not allowed to leave the Soviet Union. I recall Secretary of State George Schultz when he said that whenever he met with his Soviet counterpart, and from him down to the lowest level State Department officer, he would bring with him a list of imprisoned dissidents and human rights advocates. Front and center of any discussion whether at nuclear arms or tension in the Middle East, Secretary Schultz would bring up dissidents, naming them by name. It was this constant focus on human rights that helped move the Soviet Government to allow Jews and others to leave the Soviet Union, great people such as the great Natan Sharansky.

And I have another list of names I would like to read, that of six members of the Cuban National Front of Civic Resistance who have applied for visas to come to the United States, but for some reason, inexplicably, our State Department has refused to allow to visit the U.S. They are Orlando Gomez Echavarria, Jose Alberto Alvarez Bravo, Yaite Diasnell Cruz Sosa, Yoel Bravo Lopez, Lazaro Ricardo Fiallo Lopez, and Ciro Aleixis Casanova Perez. I call upon Secretary Kerry to allow these brave people to enter the United States so they can meet with all of us who want to hear their stories about what is truly happening on the ground in Cuba.

Finally, I note that the administration has failed to secure the release of fugitives from justice, such as JoAnne Chesimard, who is on the FBI's Most Wanted Terror List, convicted of killing a New Jersey State Trooper, Werner Foerster. The administration must insist upon the unconditional return of Chesimard and all other fugitives from justice, as well as demand that the Castro regime respect the civil and political rights of the Cuban people before making any further concessions. And to underscore the point, unconditional means unconditional. There should be no swap where we exchange convicted Cuban spies like Ana Montes, or Kendall Myers for these fugitives as a concession to the Castro regime. The effect of that would be to trade Americans who have committed crimes in the United States for other Americans who have committed crimes in the United States demoralizing our intelligence community further in the process.

With that, I want to turn to our witnesses. And before that, we turn to my good friend and colleague, Ms. Bass, for any opening comments she might have.

Ms. BASS. Thank you, Mr. Chair.

For me, I think I will probably sit here today and say minority in terms of what my opinions and viewpoints are. And with all due respect, especially to my colleague Albio Sires, who I know is a Cuban-American and had a terrible experience with his family and all in Cuba, but I do stand here as somebody who is happy that we have finally changed our policy in Cuba. For over 50 years having a policy that I think many people in the world viewed as a failed policy, and then our history on the island prior to 1959 was not positive, and I think in the last 50 years was not positive. The numerous attempts that have been—there are the numerous incidents that have been documented of the U.S. trying to overthrow the Government of Cuba, versus the Cuban people standing up, attempts by the CIA to assassinate Cuban leaders. There was the suspect plane that was shot down in the mid-1970s in which an entire athletic team was lost, a Cuban plane. And now we have President Obama who on December 17 finally changed our policy. Many countries around the world disagreed with our policy for many years. The embargo that we had really limited a lot of trade with Cuba, but over the years, especially the last 20 years, a lot of countries began ignoring that embargo, and I think we looked rather strange, especially in the Americas. So the President reestablishing diplomatic relations while removing Cuba as a designation as a State Sponsor of Terrorism, increasing travel and commerce; I, frankly, have always felt that as a U.S. citizen I should have the right to travel anywhere in the world I choose to travel. The increase in remittances and trade and communications, the idea of U.S. companies beginning to have a physical presence on the island. We do know that the embargo still remains, and I'm hoping over time we lift that embargo.

One concern I have in terms of Afro-Cubans that you mentioned is, I know that because of the remittances, not everybody has family here that can give remittances to their family members on the island. And maybe it's time we reconsider some of our other policies. For example, we provide a lot of U.S. support to media that is supposed to go into Cuba, but as I understand it, the Cuban Government blocks, and so I wonder what is happening with all of those resources. And maybe those resources could be redirected to help address some of the inequities in Cuba, especially with the Afro-Cuban population and the population that does not have the access to remittances.

Again, I welcome my colleague here, Mr. Sires from New Jersey, and more than willing to share with the approval of the chair my time with him, so I would yield to my colleague.

Mr. SMITH. I would yield such time as it may consume to Albio Sires, a good friend and colleague from New Jersey.

Mr. SIRES. Thank you, Mr. Chairman, Ranking Member Bass. Thank you very much, and thank you for allowing me to participate with you today, both chairman and ranking member. And for holding this important hearing, and for allowing me to attend.

It has been 18 months since our relationship with Cuba has changed, and what continues to trouble me is that for all the talk of additional actions to be taken by the United States, little has been said of the steps the Cuban regime must take. Far too much has been given already. We need to see more concrete measures in terms of human rights, political freedoms, and the release of all political prisoners.

People are routinely jailed and innocent women are beaten, while Castro continues to harbor dangerous fugitives, including JoAnne Chesimard, one of the FBI's Most Wanted individuals for killing a New Jersey State Trooper, and then fleeing her prison sentence to live out her days on the island.

What also upsets me is that while the Castro regime continues to oppress innocent people, he will be able to strengthen his grip on power by pocketing all the tourism dollars that the U.S. engagement will bring into the state-owned businesses further depriving the Cuban people an opportunity at a better life.

We need to do more to bring attention to the plight of the Cuban people and implore our neighbors to stand up to the Castro regime and speak out against the continued human rights violation.

I thank my colleagues once again for holding this important hearing, and I urge the administration to finally make human rights in Cuba a top priority. Thank you.

Mr. SMITH. Mr. Sires, thank you very much, and I thank you for your leadership on human rights in general, but especially as it relates to Cuba. You have been tenacious, and I want to note that Mario Diaz-Balart was here earlier and when he served here and now out of office in like manner does the same great work. And Kristina Arriaga, I want to thank her. As some of you saw, she was sworn in earlier right before the hearing. She from being one of the leaders of the Becket Fund to the United States Commission for International Religious Freedom as one of the commissioners. And I look forward to her work on the Commission, and then the entire commission as we go forward.

Is Lincoln still here? I guess Lincoln has left, but he was a great leader like his brother, Mario.

Let me just introduce our very distinguished group of witnesses, people for whom, and I believe this subcommittee has just such great respect for beginning with Dr. Oscar Biscet, who was born in Havana. In 1987, he began practicing the medical profession and teaching at the hospital in Havana. Dr. Biscet openly opposed Cuba's communist regime and in 1994, Cuban authorities opened an official case where he was accused of carrying out ''dangerous activities.''

Dr. Biscet was arrested in 1999, and officially accused of crimes such as dishonoring national symbols, disorderly contact and inciting delinquent conduct. These are obviously catchall phrases so often employed against dissidents. As a result of these accusations he was sentenced to 3 years in prison. After his release in 2002 he was rearrested but later released thanks to pressure from religious and human rights organizations.

He received the Presidential Medal of Freedom from President George Bush. While this is Dr. Biscet's first time appearing before the subcommittee in person, he offered dramatic testimony, as I mentioned earlier before to the subcommittee in February 2012 when he testified via telephone from the U.S. Interests Section in Havana.

We'll then hear from Ms. Sirley Avila Leon who is an ex-delegate of the People's Assembly. She joined the democratic opposition after she was driven out of her position for trying to keep a school open in her community. Official channels ignored her and after she went to the international media, she was removed from office.

Following escalating acts of repression by state security, she was gravely wounded in a machete attack in May 2015, in what was believed to have been an officially sanctioned attempt on her life.

In September 2015, the Inter-American Commission on Human Rights concurred that she was in a ''serious and urgent situation since her life and physical integrity are at risk.'' In March 2016, she arrived in the U.S. to tell her compelling story and to obtain medical care.

We'll then hear from Ms. Maria Werlau who co-founded in 2012 and still heads the Free Society Project, a nonprofit organization to advance human rights through research and scholarship. Its leading initiative, the Cuba Archive Truth and Memory Project focuses on transitional justice issues and human exploitation.

Ms. Werlau is a former Second Vice President of Chase Manhattan Bank and a longtime independent consultant specializing in Cuban affairs and other international issues. Her extensive publications on Cuba cover a wide range of topics, including policy, international law, foreign investment, and other economic issues. She has served task forces on U.S.-Cuban relations for the Council on Foreign Relations and the American Enterprise Institute.

And then we'll hear from Mr. Geoff Thale. Mr. Thale oversees the entire range of the Washington Office on Latin America's research and advocacy, on Latin American policy, and human rights issues, along with a focus on specific countries and themes. Mr. Thale led the team that authored ''Forging New Ties,'' as well as recommendations for new directions in U.S. policy toward Latin America.

Mr. Thale has studied Cuba issues since the mid-1990s, and has traveled to Cuba more than a dozen times, including organizing delegations of academics and Members of Congress. He coordinates WOLA's advocacy on this issue with a coalition of business, agricultural, and human rights groups who favor lifting the travel ban and rebuilding contacts between the United States and Cuban society.

Dr. Biscet, the floor is yours.

STATEMENT OF OSCAR ELIAS BISCET, M.D., PRESIDENT, LAWTON FOUNDATION FOR HUMAN RIGHTS (FORMER CUBAN POLITICAL PRISONER)

[The following testimony was delivered through an interpreter.]

Dr. BISCET. Good afternoon. Thank you for the opportunity to address you on behalf of the suffering people of Cuba. This subcommittee of the House directed by Congressman Christopher Smith has been an unshakeable bastion of the promotion and defense of the freedom values of the American nation. These values that ennoble human dignity for those whose rights are violated flagrantly and systematically in my nation.

In my country, Cuba, a small group of individuals using criminal conduct have taken over the administrative power and through state terror have kidnaped the sovereignty and freedom of the people and set up a society of fear. For more than 57 years the basic human rights, the freedom to talk, freedom of the press, to gather, association, and religious freedom have been undermined against the dignity of my people.

The socialist regime that rules my country run first by Fidel Castro, now by his brother, Raul, was imposed by force with the use of weapons of war and overrode the 1940 Constitution. This Constitution was suspended de facto, never abolished de jure; that is why even in theory it is still in force and it declares the Castro communist regime as illegitimate.

The 1940 Constitution guarantees the freedom and the human rights of the Cuban people through its Letter of Rights in Chapter IV. This letter was inspired in the American Bill of Rights of the United States Constitution of 1788, that strengthens modern democracy in the world starting with its cry of independence in 1776.

Actually, the Obama administration has established diplomatic relations with the dictatorship in Communist Cuba violating the Act for Freedom and Cuban Solidarity, or known also as the Helms-Burton Law. But worst of all was the undermining of the American values of freedom enshrined in the Bill of Rights of its Constitution.

Admirable Mr. Smith, Congresspersons, excellencies, I'm here today to highlight the honorable example of George Mason and Patrick Henry in the Congress of the State of Virginia where they firmly opposed to countersign the Constitution of the United States until the Bill of Rights was introduced. Congresspersons, don't allow that the creed of a nation, the Bill of Rights, continue to be violated flagrantly. Don't be tolerant maintaining the American and Cuban people separated in two nations, yours free, and mine, Cuba, slave. With your solidarity you not only enhance human dignity, but you accelerate the process through which democracy and freedom comes to the Cuban people.

Thank you very much. God bless America and Cuba.

[The prepared statement of Dr. Biscet follows:]

Testimony of Dr. Oscar Elias Biscet, delivered in English by John Suarez

In the Subcommittee of Africa, Global Health, Global Human Rights, and International Organizations

Of the House of Representatives of the United States of America

This committee of the house directed by the Congressman Christopher Smith has been an unshakable bastion of the promotion and defense of the freedom values on the American nation. These values that ennoble the human dignity are those who are violated flagrantly and systematically in my nation.

In my country, Cuba, a small group of individuals with delinquent conduct have taken over the administrative power and through the state terror have kidnapped the sovereign and the freedom of the people and have set up a society of fear. For more than 57 years the basic human rights: the freedom to talk, press, gathering, association and religious, had been undermined against the dignity of my people.

The socialist regime that rules my country, directed first by Fidel Castro, and now, by his Brother Raul, was set up by the force of the war weapons and override the 1940's Constitution. This was suspended de facto and never abolished of jure; that is why even in theory is still in force and it declares the Castro - communist regime as illegitimate.

The 1940's Constitution warranties the freedom and the human rights of the Cuban People through its Letter of rights in Chapter IV. This Letter was inspired in the American Bill of Rights of the Constitution of the United States of 1788, that strengthens the modern Democracy in the world, starting with its Cry of Independence in 1776.

Actually, the Executive US Administration, stablished diplomatic relations with the Dictatorship in Communist Cuba, violating the Act for Freedom and Cuban Solidarity or Hems-Burton's Law. But the worst of all was: the undermining of the American values of freedom of the Bill of Rights of its Constitution.

Admirable Mr. Smith, Congresspersons, excellencies: I'm here today to highlight the honorable pennant of George Mason and Patrick Henry in the Congress of the State of Virginia, where they firmly opposed to countersign the Constitution of the United States until was introduced the Letter of Rights. Congresspersons don't allow that the Creed of a Nation, the Bill of Rights, continue to be violated flagrantly, don't be tolerant maintaining the American and Cuban people apart in two nations, yours Free, and mine, Cuba, Slave. With your solidarity you not only enhance the human dignity, but you accelerate the process through the democracy and freedom of the Cuban people.

Thank you very much, God bless America, and Cuba.

Mr. SMITH. Dr. Biscet, thank you so very, very much. I'd like to now turn to Ms. Avila, and please present your testimony.

STATEMENT OF MS. SIRLEY AVILA LEON, DEMOCRACY ADVOCATE

[The following testimony was delivered through an interpreter.]

Ms. AVILA LEON. My name is Sirley Avila Leon. I am Cuban, and I live in Cuba. Because of my work as a delegate to the Municipal Assembly of People's Power for the Majibacoa municipality since 2005 I have perceived, have seen the double standards of our leaders who in reality are not interested in the people. The biggest problems were bureaucratic. There was so much corruption that the system did not work.

From the beginning, I started to take interest in the lives of the citizens and, in particular, the children of my region who walked more than 9 kilometers through difficult roads in order to attend the nearest school. The parents needing to accompany their children had no time to cultivate their land despite the abject poverty in which they lived. Some emmigrated to other villages in order to spare their children. I set myself to the task of demanding the school that the neighborhood needed so much. I reached the highest echelons of power in Cuba passing through all the intermediate levels, and although I managed to get a school built, it was soon closed leaving the village and rural children in the same situation of helplessness.

Because of my work and my demands in favor of reopening the school, I began to be accused of being a leader, and the families of the farmers in my area began to receive threats that their school-age children would be taken away from them. I was threatened and repeatedly repressed by government officials, and in Havana I was even expelled from the Council of State and threatened with being accused of threatening state security.

All this is what led me on September 8, 2012 to denounce the regime's human rights violations against the farmers and the people in general from the island itself by means of the broadcast Radio Marti. From that moment onwards I was a victim of several attempts on my life, attempts to eliminate me physically and other acts of vandalism against my farm, my animals, and my property all organized by the regime and its political police as part of its attempt to get rid of me.

A young woman, Yudisleidy Lopez Rodriguez, alerted me to the fact that the political police had offered highly dangerous common criminals rewards for murdering me. She was killed on September 26, 2014 for publicly decrying an attack on me in which my bed was set on fire during the early morning. Her murder was covered up as a crime of passion.

On May 24, 2015, I was attacked in my home by Osmani Carrion, who was sent by state security to kill me. I am sure he was sent by the political police because I later discovered that he was a highly dangerous common prisoner who had been granted parole only days before attacking me. He attacked me with a machete severing my left hand and mutilating my right arm and both knees. He did not cut off my head thanks to the presence of a child at the scene of the events, and thanks to God who protected my life so that I could be here today and offer my testimony. In the days before the attack the regime had started a rumor that I had sold the farm and had left the area so that the neighbors would not be concerned about my physical disappearance. And I am sure of this because today marks the 22nd anniversary of the sinking of the 13 de Marzo tugboat that claimed the lives of 37 men, women, and children.

Today before this subcommittee of the Committee on Foreign Affairs and the United States Congress I want to ask two questions. Taking into account the U.S. Government's new relations with the dictatorship of Cuba, I wonder why has the situation of systematic human rights violations in Cuba not been a fundamental point in negotiations with the regime that has been in power for 57 years? How is it possible that the U.S. Government has made so many concessions to the regime of Cuba without demanding respect for human rights on the island, and justice for the many attacks on the civil and political rights of the Cuban people? I am a direct witness of the workings of the legal system in which citizens are not guaranteed any procedural safeguards.

I am very grateful that over the years other victims of repression in Cuba have had the chance to come forward in this very space in order to denounce and publicize the realities of life in Cuba, and I thank you for giving me the opportunity to participate here today. I ask only that the Government of the United States, international human rights organizations, and the governments of the free world not abandon the people of Cuba in their struggle for freedom. Do not allow yourselves to be confused by the regime's propaganda campaign presenting Cuba as a country in transition. Cuba remains a military dictatorship. In Cuba, human rights continue to be violated, and the people of Cuba are now more alone than ever behind the curtain of foreign investors and North American tourists. I ask you not to abandon Cuba and to denounce the harsh reality we live. Thank you very much.

[The prepared statement of Ms. Avila Leon follows:]

Written Statement
By Sirley Avila Leon, Human Rights Activist
For the Committee on Foreign Affairs and the
Subcommittee on Africa, Global Health, Global Human Rights, and International
Organizations
on the occasion of the upcoming hearing on
July 13, 2016: The Castro Regime's Ongoing Violations of Civil and Political Rights
Text translated by John Suarez

My name is Sirley Avila Leon, I'm Cuban and I live in Cuba. Since 2005 because of my work as a delegate to the Municipal Assembly of People's Power for the Majibacoa municipality I saw the double standards of the leaders who were not really interested in the people. The biggest problems were bureaucratic, because of so much corruption, the system did not work. From the beginning, I became interested in the lives of the citizens and for the children in my area, who walked more than 9 kilometers through difficult roads, to attend the nearest school. The parents to accompany their children did not have time to cultivate the land despite the abject poverty in which they lived. Some so as to sacrifice less of their children migrated to other villages. I gave myself the task of reclaiming the school much needed in the neighborhood. I reached the highest echelons of power in Cuba, passing through all the intermediate levels, and although I managed to get a school built, it was soon closed leaving the village and rural children in the same situation of helplessness.

For my work and demands in favor of reopening the school I started to be accused of being a leader and to the families of the farmers in my area they began to threaten to take their school age children away. I was threatened and repeatedly repressed by government officials and even in Havana I was expelled from the Council of State and threatened with being accused of threatening State Security. It was for all this stated before that I turned up on September 8, 2012 through Radio Marti, from the island, to denounce violations of human rights committed by the regime against the farmers and the people in general. From that moment I was a victim of several attempts on my life, attempts to physically eliminate me and other vandalism against my farm, animals and property, all organized by the regime and its political police, in an attempt to get rid of me. A young woman, Yudisleidy Lopez Rodriguez, warned me that the political police had offered a bounty to highly dangerous common prisoners for killing me. She was killed on September 26, 2014 for publicly denouncing it after I suffered an attack where they burned my bed in the early morning. Her murder was disguised as a crime of passion.

On May 24, 2015, I was attacked in my home by Osmani Carrión, sent by State Security to kill me. I am sure he was sent by the political police because after the fact I discovered that Carrion Osmani was a highly dangerous common prisoner who days before assaulting me had been granted parole. He attacked me with a machete cutting off my left hand, mutilating my right arm and both knees. He did not cut off my head thanks to the presence of a child at the scene, and to God who protected my life to be here today and give my testimony. In the days before the attack the regime had started a rumor that I had sold the farm and had left the area with the intention that the neighbors would not be preoccupied with my physical disappearance.

Today before this Subcommittee of Foreign Affairs of the United States Congress I want to ask two questions. Taking into account the U.S. government's new relations with the dictatorship of Cuba, I wonder:

Why has the situation of systematic human rights violations in Cuba not been a fundamental point in negotiations with the regime that has been 57 years in power?

How is it possible that the US government has made so many concessions to the government of Cuba without demanding respect for human rights on the island and justice for the many attacks on civil and political rights of Cubans? I am a direct witness of the manner in which the legal system functions where there are no procedural safeguards for citizens.

I am very grateful that over the years, other victims of repression in Cuba have presented themselves and have had this space to denounce and make known the Cuban reality. And I thank you for giving me the opportunity to participate here today. I just ask the government of the United States, international human rights organizations, and the governments of the free world not to abandon the people of Cuba in their struggle for freedom. Do not allow yourselves to be confused by the regime's propaganda campaign presenting Cuba as a country in transition. Cuba remains a military dictatorship, in Cuba human rights continue to be violated, and at this moment the people of Cuba are more alone than ever behind the curtain of foreign investors and North American tourists.

I ask you not to abandon Cuba and that our harsh reality be denounced.

Thank you very much.

Mr. SMITH. Ms. Avila, thank you so very much for your testimony and for suffering personal injury for your beliefs, and your testimony was outstanding.

I'd like to now ask Ms. Werlau if you could present your testimony, as well.

STATEMENT OF MS. MARIA WERLAU, PRESIDENT, FREE SOCIETY PROJECT

Ms. WERLAU. Thank you, Mr. Chairman and members of the subcommittee for the opportunity to offer you this testimony. Please consider for the record my more extensive written statement.

Mr. SMITH. Without objection it will be made part of the record.

Ms. WERLAU. Thank you.

Today I will focus on the Cuban Government's continuing violations of the right to life. To illustrate the extreme contempt for human life the Castro regime has displayed from its inception, we need just recall three of its flagrant atrocities that occurred on the month of July of different years.

In 1994, on a day like today, July 13, a group of 68, including many women and children, boarded a tugboat to escape to the United States. Three boats were waiting for them, alerted by infiltrators. With high-pressure water jets, they began ripping children from their parents arms and sweeping terrified passengers off to sea. Finally, they rammed and sunk the fleeing tugboat, drowning all those who had taken refuge in the cargo hold. With survivors clinging to pieces of wreckage, the pursuing boats then circled around them seeking to drown them with wave turbulence. Thirty-seven perished including 11 children.

Fourteen years earlier, on July 6, 1980, Cuban Navy boats and an air force plane had attacked an excursion boat that toured the Canimar River of Matanzas loaded with passengers who tried to flee to the United States. The exact number of victims from that massacre is unknown, but numbers in the dozens and included children.

Among hundreds of July victims of the Castros, two stand out. On July 22nd, 2012, Oswaldo Paya, arguably Cuba's leading opposition figure, and Harold Cepero, a young activist from his organization, were killed in a car accident believed to have been caused by state agents. These are just examples of the large-scale and growing tragedy the Cuba Archive Project, which I head, is documenting and for which the Cuban regime has not been held accountable.

To date, we've recorded over 6,100 deaths and disappearances caused by the Castro regime—or so attributed to the Castro regime by our Project—not from combat situations. Each has a detailed record. The victims include infants, pregnant women, the elderly, human rights defenders, Protestant pastors, Jehovah's Witnesses, political prisoners, young men objecting to military service, and anyone who gets in the way of the Castros. Also on the list are 21 U.S. citizens executed, assassinated, or disappeared, and six killed in terrorist attacks sponsored or supported by Cuba.

We know, sadly, that this count is woefully lacking. What's more, for it to be comprehensive it would have to include many more Cubans who have perished and extended to many countries where

Cuba has created, supported, and promoted wars, subversion, and terrorism as today in nearby Venezuela and Colombia. The human toll of the Castro dynasty is easily, in my view, several hundred thousand and counting.

Things are not much better since Raul Castro, until 10 years ago the number two man, assumed supreme command in Cuba, replacing his brother, Fidel. Since then and until last December 31st, Cuba Archive has documented 264 cases of death and disappearance, a count we know is very incomplete.

A particularly troubling aspect of the ongoing crimes of the Cuba regime relates to the grave abuses committed by Cuban authorities against persons attempting to escape the country. The attacks appear to have declined, in part because Cuba has perfected a highly lucrative business from exporting people that welcomes most departures; yet killings, beatings, torture, and other abuses perpetrated on those fleeing have not stopped.

To take just one example, on December 16, 2014, the day before President Obama made his surprise announcement of normalizing relations with Cuba, 32-year-old Liosbel Diaz disappeared after Cuban border guards sunk, reportedly in international waters, the boat in which he was escaping with 31 passengers, including women and children.

What's perhaps more egregious is the aberration of a tropical Berlin Wall at Guantanamo, altogether overlooked by the free world. Twenty-six years after the fall of the infamous Berlin Wall, a deadlier replica now lasting twice longer stands in Communist Cuba. Barbed wire, mine fields, watch towers, ferocious dogs, sharpshooters, all to prevent escapes to the U.S. base in Guantanamo. It has a sordid extension, a sea wall in the Bay added in the mid-1990s to prevent swimmers from reaching the U.S. base.

Cuba Archive has documented several dozen individuals killed or disappeared while attempting to flee to our base in Guantanamo, but we believe that hundreds, perhaps thousands have paid with their lives, limbs, eyes, or years of prison for attempting the crossing in the last 5½ decades. Our Government is well aware of the land mines on the Cuban side and that the Cuban guards stationed around our base have orders to shoot to kill the fence jumpers.

Let me finish with an important clarification. Our work is not primarily about lists or statistics. Each number or name on these lists, or the victims missing from them, is a story, a stolen life, a circle of loved ones left behind in grief, and to date without foreseeable justice. We try to honor each person by gathering as much information as possible and dedicating an individual record of our database to each one, but it is impossible to have a full tally of the magnitude of this tragedy, and much less to convey the loss and suffering connected to each story, or to this overall calamity. At times, it overwhelms.

I urge you to visit our Web site, CubaArchive.org, and familiarize yourself with these stories, at least see some of the faces, as we have pictures of many victims. The Cuban regime is guilty of egregious, extensive, and ongoing crimes against humanity. This is an amply documented fact that reputable governments and institutions, as well as principled individuals can only ignore at will. I firmly believe that continuing to afford the Cuban Government impunity and engaging it on its terms only produces more victims and provides resources for its tyrannical ways. That is not just bad for the Cuban people, the imprint of this regime is exported globally with the help of rogue allies, and that is to the detriment of our security and of global freedom and peace. Thank you.

[The prepared statement of Ms. Werlau follows:]

The Castro Regime's Ongoing Violations of Civil and Political Rights

Testimony of
Maria C. Werlau
President, Free Society Project

Committee on Foreign Affairs, U.S. House of Representatives, Washington, DC
Subcommittee on Africa, Global Health, Global Human Rights, and
International Organizations - Christopher H. Smith (R-NJ), Chairman
Wednesday, July 13, 2016 - 2:00PPM
Rayburn House Office Building

The Cuban regime, never legitimized by a free election in its 57 years in power, has managed to secure near absolute impunity from the international community as well as increasing legitimacy and support. This should not surprise given its decades-long and vast dedication of resources to wielding influence and spreading propaganda. Yet, that it is a totalitarian dictatorship guilty of egregious, widespread, and ongoing crimes against humanity is an amply documented fact that reputable governments and institutions or principled individuals can only ignore at will.

The Cuban government violates –both in practice and in the letter of Cuba's laws —most universally recognized civil and political rights. We could dedicate many hearings just to touch on the systemic abuse to freedom of speech, association, press, or the denial of basic political rights' such as self-determination, not to mention the suppression of economic and cultural rights. But, for lack of time, I will focus today on the violations of the right to life, as I head a project, Cuba Archive (www.CubaArchive.org), dedicated to this issue.

Since its beginnings in January 1959 and to this day, the Castro regime has repeatedly demonstrated its contempt for human life. July is particularly significant, as it is the anniversary month of three flagrant atrocities perpetrated by Cuban authorities; they have gone mostly unrecognized and altogether unpunished, as the rest of the Castro regime's crimes --individual and mass murders-- taking place any month of any year.

The Canimar River Massacre occurred on July 6, 1980 after three youngsters hijacked an excursion boat; its passengers immediately celebrated the opportunity to escape Cuba for the United States. Cuban Navy patrol boats and an Air Force plane opened fire on the vessel, injuring and killing many, then rammed it until it sank. The number of victims is unconfirmed (there was capacity for one hundred passengers) and includes children, none of the recovered bodies were returned to their families for burial. The ten survivors were threatened into silence and kept under constant surveillance for years.

Fourteen years later, in 1994 and on a day like today, July 13th, a group of sixty-eight that included many children boarded a tugboat in the middle of the night hoping to escape to the United States. They where chased by three waiting tugboats --alerted by infiltrators, as is common in Cuba-- that began spraying the escapees with high-pressure water jets, sweeping terrified passengers off to sea and ripping children from their parents' arms. Finally, the tugboat was rammed and sunk. Passengers who had taken refuge in the cargo hold were pinned down and wailed until they drowned. The three pursuing tugboats circled around survivors who clung to pieces of wreckage, creating wave turbulence to drown them too. The attack stopped suddenly and survivors were pulled from the water only after a merchant ship with Greek flag approached Havana that could have borne witness. Thirty-seven perished, including eleven children, none of the bodies were returned to their families for burial. Male survivors were detained for months and given psychotropic drugs. All survivors and relatives of the deceased were put under surveillance, fired from their jobs and harassed systematically. Eventually, most left for exile.[1]

To cite just two more cases from our list of hundreds of victims for the month, on July 22nd 2012, Cuban opposition leader Oswaldo Payá, of the Christian Liberation Movement, and a youth leader from his group, Harold Cepero, died after a car accident the New York-based Human Rights Foundation "strongly suggests" was "directly caused by agents of the state.[2]

The above are but a small sample of the large-scale tragedy that Cuba Archive is attempting to document. As of December 31, 2015 our work-in-process had documented over 6,200 cases of death and disappearance attributed to the Castro regime not resulting from combat operations; these include over 3,100 persons executed without due process of law. The victims include small children, pregnant women, elderly persons, human rights' advocates, protestant pastors, Jehovah's Witnesses, homosexuals, young men objecting to the obligatory military service, exported workers put to work in unsafe and crime-infested, and anyone who gets in the way or unintentionally happens to fall prey of the Cuban regime's Stalinist laws and practices. The ghastly list also includes 43 U.S. citizens, 21 reported as executed, assassinated, or disappeared and 6 killed in terrorist attacks sponsored or supported by Cuba (there are likely many more). [3]

We know, sadly, that this count is but a sample of the many more victims of the Cuban regime who remain nameless or simply have not yet been documented. It would extend to numerous countries in Africa, Latin America, the Middle East and, actually, around the globe, where Cuba has created, supported, and promoted war, subversion and terror, including today in nearby Venezuela. The human toll of the Castro dynasty is easily, in my view, several hundred thousand. It's critical to remember that each victim, no matter their nationality, has a name, a face, a story, loved ones left behind in grief, and, at least for now, without any hope of justice.

---

[1] More detailed accounts of both massacres are available at www.CubaArchive.org, Reports.
[2] The complete report can be found at http://humanrightsfoundation.org/news/cuba-hrf-report-on-oswaldo-payas-death-evidence-suggests-government-may-have-killed-him-00446
[3] See "U.S. Citizens Killed or Disappeared by Cuba's Communist Regime: 43, Update of June 26 2016," www.CubaArhive.org (Reports).

Today, the Cuban government does not kill its people en masse as it did in its early years. That's bad public relations. The application of capital punishment is on hold since three young men were executed for trying to steal a ferry in 2003 to escape the island. Yet, there are persons on death row and dozens of causes for capital punishment in the Penal Code, most for crimes to state security. Just as in the former Communist regimes of East Germany (German Democratic Republic), Poland, Czechoslovakia, and others, once armed uprisings had been defeated --in Cuba, by the late 1960s--, terror implanted and the repressive apparatus well in place, fear together with more sophisticated means of control are deemed sufficient to keep the rulers in power. The Cuban police state has, in fact, proven exceptionally successful; its huge counterintelligence machinery for internal control has, according to defectors, a higher surveillance ratio than that of all former Soviet bloc countries. Cuba's intelligence services is one of the most dedicated and effective in the world; while the population has been subjected to misery and food rations for decades, the "Dirección de Inteligencia" has always had plenty of resources to advance Cuba's goals internationally.

In the surviving archives of the former Soviet bloc countries, there is evidence of the shared methodology of control and of the operational links between the secret police of Cuba and that of all the iron curtain countries. The archives of the former East German Stasi, for example, reveal that it provided Cuba training and support on refined methods of torture and repression to avoid killing or executing opponents and political prisoners, just as the Stasi had accomplished in Germany.

Regardless, a steady staple of extrajudicial and other killings have been a fact since the Castro regime's inception; Cuba Archive had documented 1,166 to December 31, 2015. Things are not much better since Raúl Castro assumed supreme command in Cuba ten years ago after his brother Fidel retired for health reasons.[4] Since then, from July 2006, and to December 31, 2015, Cuba Archive had documented (in what is considered a very partial count) 264 cases of death and disappearance, including 2 forced disappearances, 34 extrajudicial killings, 6 deaths from protest hunger strikes in prison, 98 deaths from the denial of medical care or a medical condition developed in prison, and 52 suicides or induced/alleged suicides in prison. (See Annex 1 as well as "The Human Toll of Raúl Castro's Rule, Update of December 30, 2014" in www.CubaArchive.org, Reports.)

These numbers are only of cases properly documented. There is insufficient data on many more deaths and disappearances reported at sea in exit attempts, plus reports of deaths in prison are very limited while many are believed to be dying in the prisons, especially young men serving time for "economic crimes," not considered crimes in any civilized country.[5]

---

[4] On July 31st 2006, Fidel suddenly fell ill and Raúl, second-in-command (then First Vice President of the Council of State and Minister of Defense), was designated President of the Council of State in an intended temporary transfer of power. Fidel did not return to power and, on February 24, 2008, Raúl was officially "elected" President by the National Assembly; on April 19, 2011, he was designated First Secretary of the Communist Party at the 6th Party Congress, effectively completing the succession.

[5] Cuba Archive documents deaths of non-political prisoners given the criminalization in Cuba of many activities that contravene universally accepted human rights' standards, the absence of due process of law or of international monitoring, and because reporting from inside the prisons leads to reprisals.

There is one particularly troubling aspect of the ongoing killings by the Cuban regime I would like to highlight --the abuses, including killings, committed against persons attempting to escape the country, including the aberration that is, in my view, Cuba's "Berlin Wall" at Guantánamo.

Cuba passed regulations relaxing very harsh travel restrictions beginning January 2013, but its Article 215 of the Penal Code continues to forbid the citizens from leaving the country without prior government authorization. Attempting to do so is punishable with years of prison. Stealing or hijacking a vessel to flee can lead to capital punishment.

Cuba Archive has documented, as of July 11, 2016, the following for attempting to escape the country: 156 extrajudicial killings, 24 executions, and 14 forced disappearances, all perpetrated by the Cuban state. In addition, we have documented 902 disappearances, but many could well be forced disappearances or killings by state actors. The actual number of victims of attempts to escape Cuba, including those drowning, dying of exposure, and devoured by sharks, is estimated in the tens of thousands.

Attacks by Cuban authorities on people fleeing Cuba have reportedly declined to a great degree, as Castro, Inc. has gradually developed and now perfected a highly lucrative business of exporting its people that welcomes most departures. But, the killings and abuses have not altogether stopped.

On December 16, 2014, the day before President Obama made his surprise announcement on normalization of relations with Cuba, 32 year-old Liosbel Díaz Beoto disappeared after Cuban Boarder Guards sunk the boat in which he was traveling with 31 other passengers, including seven women and two children. Survivors insisted they had been in international waters 22 miles away from the coast of Matanzas, Cuba, from where they had left. For two hours, the border guards shot at and rammed the boat until it sunk, as the passengers screamed begging for mercy. Liosbel had gone back to Cuba attempting to smuggle out of the island his wife and 5 year-old son.

On April 8, 2015, 30-year old Yurinieski Martinez Reina was killed by a State Security agent at a beach in Matanzas after the agent fired on a group of five who had attempted to leave Cuba on a homemade raft. In June 2015, fourteen Cubans boarded a tugboat in Santiago de Cuba and, with the agreement of the captain and all the passengers, headed for the United States. Having reached international waters and around 38 miles from the island, they were intercepted by a Cuban Border Guard vessel that, without warning, began to ram the tugboat. The border guards then boarded the fleeing tugboat and began to brutally beat the passengers, including the women. Brought back to Cuba in very bad condition from the beatings, the passengers were carried to a military hospital for treatment and then taken to a detention center known as "Versalles," feared for the physical and psychological torture dispensed there. Kept incommunicado in dark, hot, and pestilent cells with no ventilation or sanitary facilities with no water for bathing, and sleeping on dirty floors, they were interrogated day and night, they were released after being imposed fines of 10,000 pesos, equivalent to around twenty times the average monthly wage, which by the way, is ranked the lowest in the world.[6] Five were fined 1000 pesos a day until their trial, or twice the average monthly wage.[7] This is a new modality of Raúl's reforms, huge fines instead of prison, another way to cash in from repression.

What's perhaps even more egregious is that, while the infamous Berlin Wall fell 26 years ago, a deadlier replica more than twice in age remains in Communist Cuba, yet remains virtually ignored. Barbed wire, high fences, minefields, watchtowers, ferocious dogs, and sharpshooters firing at unarmed civilians..., this tropical version of "The Wall" prevents escapees from reaching the U.S. naval base in Guantánamo. There is even a distinctive extension of the barrier into Guantánamo Bay --a sea wall built in the mid-1990s (visible on Google Earth) with a net allowing authorized maritime traffic, surrounded by border guards firing from patrol boats or throwing grenades at anyone trying to swim towards the U.S. base.

During the 28-year existence of the Berlin Wall (1961-1989), 227 persons were killed attempting to cross to West Berlin. Cuba Archive has documented 34 confirmed cases of individuals killed or disappeared while attempting to flee to the U.S. Guantánamo Naval base, 6 more killed by mines and 39 other reported cases lacking confirmation. (See Annex II for a list and a more detailed report at CubaArchive.org, Reports.) We know from human rights' defenders in Guantánamo as well as from numerous accounts, that 57 years of the Cuban version of the wall have seen countless hundreds, perhaps thousands paying with their lives, limbs, eyes, or years of prison for attempting the crossing. The mother of a 26 year-old shot January 1994 as he swam unarmed towards the base hoping to obtain asylum, has told me about a large field of unmarked graves at the cemetery in Guantánamo --on the Cuban side-- for victims of foiled escape attempts to the base. Photos of the two victims riveted with bullets were exhibited in a Guantánamo school to warn against escaping and facing a similar fate. The two sharpshooters who with long-range automatic rifles killed her son, Iskander Maleras, and his friend, Luis Angel Valverde, from their watchtower were commended in a ceremony for doing their duty.

Successive U.S. administrations, although usually granting refuge to those who make it to the base, have kept largely silent on this killing field in order to —I have been told—- avoid provoking the Castros and having the base overrun by asylum seekers. Our government is well aware that Cuban guards stationed around the base have orders to shoot to kill "fence-jumpers" and keeps classified records of all recorded incidents. The Clinton administration reportedly filed a rare protest with the Cuban government in June 1994 after many defenseless swimmers had been attacked with grenades and shot by Cuban Border guards as they attempted to reach the base; U.S. personnel could see the bodies being fished out of the water with gaffing hooks. Raúl Castro, now President of

---

[6] See http://www.nationmaster.com/country-info/stats/Cost-of-living/Average-monthly-disposable-salary/After-tax#2014

[7] See "Detenidos y golpeados por guardafronteras cubanos, CubaNet. octubre 8, 2015," a report from Cuba on this incident.

Cuba, was Minister of Defense at the time and the Border Guard was under his direct command.

U.S. anti-personnel and anti-tank land mines that were in the buffer zone with Cuba since 1961 —considered a Cold War necessity— were removed in 1996 to uphold international agreements. Yet, the Cuban government has not signed the Ottawa Convention banning land mines and insists on keeping its mines.

All of the crimes mentioned above, and many, many more, have been deliberately ignored by the vast majority of the international community that has capitulated to Cuba's pressure and blackmail or is seeking to reap profits from so-called business opportunities offered in partnership with the Castro regime. Sadly, while the U.S. is widely condemned for its prison for accused terrorists at Guantánamo, the mined field, killings, maiming, or ghastly dungeons on the Cuban side are altogether ignored.

Engaging this criminal regime in its own terms and offering it support and credibility only fuels its tyrannical ways, exported globally with the help of rogue allies to the detriment of our security and that of the free world. We must continue to demand an end to this impunity and forcefully denounce and reject all these gross violations to human rights by the Cuban regime. The Castros should be held accountable for their crimes and the Cuban people ought to count on solidarity from civilized nations to enjoy all their rightful freedoms.

Mr. SMITH. Thank you very much, Ms. Werlau.

And I'd like to now go to Mr. Thale.

STATEMENT OF MR. GEOFF THALE, PROGRAM DIRECTOR, WASHINGTON OFFICE ON LATIN AMERICA

Mr. THALE. Thank you, Mr. Chairman, thank you, Mr. Sires and Ms. Bass, as well, for the opportunity to speak here. I will probably present, as Ms. Bass said, something of a minority view on the panel.

I'm the Program Director of the Washington Office on Latin America. We look at human rights and social justice issues in the hemisphere. I have followed Cuba issues since the mid-1990s, and I've traveled there about three dozen times. We have a pretty broad set of contacts from Cuban Government officials through academics, the religious community, and to people in the dissident community.

I think we heard on this panel a set of very serious and real concerns about the human rights situation in Cuba. There are serious and real human rights problems on the island; although, I probably wouldn't paint them in as uniformly grim a way as some of the other panelists here would. But I think the question is less about the specifics of the situation than about how the U.S. responds to that situation. And the argument I would make is that after we have spent 56 years on an embargo and a policy regime change, this had little impact on the human rights situation on the island. Since December 17, we've made what I think is a healthy shift to a policy of engagement that over time is far more likely to make a real difference in the human rights situation in Cuba. It will give us an opportunity to project our values and our interests, and will strengthen broadly our contacts in human society.

So overall, I want to make three points, one very quickly about Cuba today, one about changes that are going on in Cuba itself, and then finally come back to the U.S. role in addressing the human rights situation and U.S. policy toward the island.

We've heard about the human rights situation in Cuba today. There are violations of freedom of speech and freedom of association. There's only one legal political party on the island. Those are real and very serious concerns. And as we've heard, there's harassment of dissidents, and though we didn't talk about it much here, pretty clearly a policy of torture and detention of dissidents.

As important for most Cubans along with the human rights situation, probably for most Cubans more important, the economy is stagnant and people, especially young people, are looking for opportunity. I don't think we should paint everything as grim in Cuba. Life expectancy is long, the medical system is reasonably good, literacy is high. There have been some efforts to address racial inequity, LGBT issues, and women's participation in the workforce. All that said, no question there are real and serious human rights in Cuba.

I think what's important, my second point here, is that there is a process of change going on on the island itself. I think we know about some of the economic changes. They are halting, there's a lot of back and forth in this process, but there's clearly movement toward the emergence of a private sector, toward greater foreign investment, and toward what eventually will be a more mixed economy in Cuba.

Along with that, and I think this has been less talked about, but I think it is evident that within Cuba itself we have seen greater political openness, and greater political debate, and greater access to and sharing of information in the last several years than we have seen in previous decades. And I think that's important.

I think we've seen the spread of cell phone technology. I think we've seen limited but real increases in Internet access. I think we've seen far more blogs and bloggers in Cuba itself expressing a much wider range of political opinions. I think we've seen the sharing through thumb drives of regular sets of information, including a lot of information from the United States, and everything from newspaper columns to the latest television shows. I think we've seen greater official tolerance of all of that behavior, and I think we've seen more debate among the nascent civil society, in the academic community, and even at official Cuban media than we have in the past. So I think there's a limited, we shouldn't exaggerate, but there's a real process of internal change going on driven in part by the economic change, driven in part by increased access to information and the internet.

In that context, the change in our relationship with Cuba is important. Before December 17th, our policy, a policy of embargo and regime change, did very little. I think if you look back, it did very little to actually encourage change on the island. In fact, more often than not, it offered the most hardlined sector in the Cuban Communist party an excuse to crack down further on dissent. I think since December 17th and under the new approach we have seen that U.S. policy interacting with changes going on on the island encourages greater openness and greater tolerance.

We heard a comment earlier about President Obama's visit, and I'd say I think President Obama's visit is actually an example of ways in which U.S. engagement helps open space. The President came, he gave a press conference. Raul Castro may or may not have responded to the question about human rights and political prisoners, but he was forced for the first time in public and on Cuban television to answer a set of uncensored questions from an international press audience. The President, our President, followed that with a nationally televised live speech in which he warmly greeted the Cuban people and made some of the strongest criticisms of the Cuban Government that they've heard on public television in many years. And then that whole visit was both preceded and followed by real debate in Cuban society, in its blogosphere, and even in the official media about what the President's visit was and meant, and what its impact has been.

So I think the argument is, in fact, our engagement rather than allowing the Cuban Government to tighten its grip, has actually helped loosen the grip, and increased flexibility, access to information, and openness. I think it's clear the President's policy and our approach to Cuba is broadly supported on the island itself. Polls show that Cubans overwhelmingly support normal relations with the United States and, in fact, that many Cuban dissidents and whatever their view of the government support normalization of U.S.-Cuban relations. It's clearly popular in the Cuban-American community here, and among U.S. population in general. And I think over time it is going to contribute to greater political openness in Cuba, and that is in our national interest and the interest of the Cuban people.

We shouldn't be naive about that process. It will be slow, it will be complicated, there will be difficulties along the way, but I think in the end the evidence is very strongly that a policy of engagement is more likely to contribute to change in the human rights situation in Cuba than the policies we've had in the past. Thanks.

[The prepared statement of Mr. Thale follows:]

Advocacy for Human Rights in the Americas

Testimony of Geoff Thale
Program Director
Washington Office on Latin America (WOLA)

House Foreign Affairs Committee
Subcommittee on Africa, Global Health, Global Human Rights,
and International Organizations

July 13, 2016

My name is Geoff Thale, and I am the Program Director at the Washington Office on Latin America, WOLA. Thank you for this invitation to testify. I know my views are somewhat different than the other witnesses, though I have the utmost respect for them, and I appreciate the opportunity to present a different viewpoint to this subcommittee.

WOLA is a U.S. non-profit, non-governmental organization that does research and advocacy to promote human rights and social justice in the Americas. Since 1974, WOLA has monitored issues of human rights and democracy in Latin America and has provided information and analysis to congressional offices, the administration, and the general public about conditions in the region and the impact of U.S. policy on human rights.

In 1995, I founded WOLA's Cuba program and have directed it ever since. I travel to Cuba every year, and have done so since the mid-1990s. I meet with a wide range of Cubans when I visit including academics, Catholic and Protestant church leaders, government officials and critics. I have met, in Havana and in Washington, with figures such as the late Oswaldo Paya and with well-known human rights activist Elisardo Sanchez, with Manuel Cuesta Morua, and with Yoani Sanchez. On recent trips, I have met with small business owners, like a young restauraunt owner in Matanzas who is representative of an emerging sector with their own interests and priorities. I have worked professionally on issues of U.S. foreign policy, human rights, and democracy in Latin America for more than 30 years.

I do not differ with my colleagues on this panel about the existence of human rights abuses in Cuba, although I do not paint as grim a picture of the problems as they do.

The real difference has more to do withwith what the United States can do to promote human rights and political opening in Cuba. For well over fifty years, the United States pursued a policy of isolation and hostility, in the expectation that it would lead to regime change and then human rights improvements in Cuba. That policy clearly failed, and in my view, the policy we are now pursuing -- normalizing diplomatic relations and seeking active engagement with Cuban society is far more likely to help create the conditions for progress on human rights in Cuba.

The United States's new posture toward Cuba doesn't guarantee human rights improvements in Cuba but it certainly opens new paths which could improve the rights situation and the living conditions of Cubans. The new policy provides opportunities to forward U.S. values and interests. Opening new avenues of engagement through travel and trade for United States individual citizens, churches, academic and cultural institutions and businesses will enhance the prospects for freedom of expression and reform on the island.

Human Rights in Cuba: Different Approaches

My colleagues on this panel have talked about their own situations and about the human rights challenges on the island. They have lived there and can describe their experiences far better than I or other foreign observers can. My expertise is focused on human rights and U.S. policy, and how U.S. policy can most effectively foster human rights improvements.

There's no doubt that Cuba has serious human rights problems. It has only one legal political party. Cuba falls short on international human rights standards on freedom of speech, freedom of the press, and freedom of association.

Perhaps as important to its citizens as the conditions listed above is Cuba's dismal economy. Although the private sector has grown substantially alongside surging tourism, Cuba's economy is overall stagnant, and many people, especially young Cubans, are yearning for more opportunity. While economic reforms have led to modest economic growth, they have led to increases in inequality, and Afro-Cuban families and youth have benefited the least from the changes underway.

To be clear, the picture in Cuba is not uniformly a grim one. Life expectancy is high, reflecting relatively good public health and medical care; literacy levels are high, reflecting universal public education. The country has made some progress on legislation to prevent discrimination based on sexual orientation. Racial inequality, which was severe in the 1950s, declined dramatically up through the 1990s. Women's participation in the workforce, particularly the professions, has improved significantly.

Yet Cuba's economic and political problems are real. However, we have started to see some shifts in recent years, and these moves in the right direction should not be ignored.

Some of the economic changes are well known -- an emerging small business and cooperative sector, private sales of homes and cars, greater openness to foreign investment.

What is less visible to outsiders are the changes in political openness.

Information is being moved around the island in ways that were unimaginable before. Although internet access is extremely limited, it is increasing, and Cubans are using it to publish blogs and articles that explore issues such as race, inequality, and lack of political options – things that would be unimaginable to have broached publicly just 10 years ago.

The *paquete*, or packet, a weekly download from a pen drive with news, apps and other media, is increasingly being sold on the island, and though technically illegal, the government tacitly allows it to be sold. While the government does still block blogs like that of Yoani Sanchez, unlike a few years ago, she and many other critical voices are not being arrested and held for long periods. There is also a small, but growing civil society that's increasingly found a voice in recent years.

The new relationship with the United States has made a positive contribution to the climate in which these changes are taking place. The reduction in hostility between the two governments has made it easier and more acceptable for people to openly debate and criticize the government.

One saw this around President Obama's visit earlier this year. For the first time, President Castro participated in a press conference with unscripted questions. President Obama gave a nationally televised speech that included explicit criticisms of the government. Before and after the visit analysis and opinion pieces circulated, including in official newspapers across the country, with levels of open debate that the country has not seen previously.

This is all not to say that there are not serious and continuing problems. Cuba should end its restrictions on political parties, freedom of speech, and freedom of assembly. While there has been more open debate than we've seen, there remains a line that cannot be crossed and certain viewpoints that are not tolerated.

One shouldn't discount the impact of new social dynamics in Cuba and how they are intersecting with the opening in US/Cuba policy. As Cubans travel abroad more freely, and Cuban Americans travel back to the island to be with family, as Cuba gradually expands internet access, as cell phone technology and pen drives proliferate, the space for debate, and the desire for information and debate, grows. There is now greater political space in Cuba and potential to grow that space. And if the past year has been any indication, the best way to encourage and facilitate this is to increase exchange and opportunities for Cubans. Continuing open exchange between the United States and Cuba, including allowing for more travel and technology, will only serve to advance and expedite this process.

The Policy of Isolation

The United States should certainly press Cuba to respect and foster human rights (though we should maintain some humility, given the troubling events that have gone on the United States in recent weeks.) The question that I will examine today, in my capacity as an analyst of U.S. foreign policy and its effect on human rights, is how best to do so.

The truth is that the last 55 years of embargo have clearly shown that our attempts to isolate Cuba completely failed to improve human rights on the island. The embargo created—and continues to create—hardships for normal Cubans, but it has not forced the Cuban government to reform. In fact, the tensions between the United States and

Cuba have long provided hardliners in the Cuban government with a pretext to crack down on dissent. Considering that isolation demonstrated no positive results, let's consider how change in Cuba is actually taking place and how engagement might encourage those changes.

The Cuban government has begun a transition. Economic changes are shifting the foundations of Cuban society, as well as the fundamentals of the relationship between Cubans and their government for the first time since the 1959 revolution. There has been a shift of large numbers of workers to the newly emerging private sector and some market mechanisms have been incorporated. Thousands of Cubans are now renting out their homes on Air BnB and as of December 2015 over 500,000 Cubans were self-employed. Given the increase in tourism that number is now significantly higher and due to increase, as small and medium-sized private businesses become legal.

So as Cuba begins a slow and halting evolution, where is the United States? Under our old policy, the United States—both its government and its citizens—was largely relegated to the sidelines.

The case for engagement

Critics of the new policy have called it a bad deal, saying that no changes have taken place in Cuba in the aftermath of the diplomatic opening. That misreads much of what has happened over the last year in the official relationship between the two governments, and it ignores the changes that are underway in Cuba itself.

More importantly however is that the previous U.S. policy achieved no results at all in this regard and in fact gave Cuban authorities cause for continuing repressive tactics. In fact, the new policy of conducting direct, high-level talks about a broad range of issues will present greater opportunity to effectively raise human rights concerns.

Engagement has proven useful in the past. President Carter dialed down the tension with Cuba and the Cuban government responded by engaging in a dialogue on political prisoners. Hundreds of political prisoners were released. Pope John Paul II visited Cuba and over the following weeks, 300 prisoners were freed. After decades of acrimony, the Archbishop of Havana, Cardinal Jaime Ortega, and Raúl Castro engaged in a series of constructive discussions. Ultimately, the dialogue resulted in the release of 110 prisoners.

Last year, we learned that 53 prisoners whose cases the United States raised with the Cuban government had been released. We understand some of the 53 released prisoners have since been detained. However, our new policy will allow the State Department to address these and other human rights challenges directly with the Cuban government.

Opening up new space for broad range of reformers

Beyond dialogue, the shift in U.S. policy has benefitted, and will continue to benefit, reformers inside the Cuban official system—in the universities and the churches, among students and the younger generation, in the new private sector—that favor greater openness. It contributes to a climate in which the emergence of debate, constructive disagreement and new ideas is more likely to happen and harder to stifle.

People-to-people exchanges and Cuban-American family travel have helped Cuban families stay connected with their relatives in the United States and receive much-needed economic support. People-to-people travelers also engage a broad range of Cubans in dialogue about politics, the economy, press freedom, health care, and a range of other issues.

Allowing U.S. telecommunications companies to operate in Cuba is helping expand internet access on the island, break down barriers to communication, and expand citizens' ability to get information and engage in debate. The reforms the United States has made will allow greater flows of non-famailial remittances. They will allow U.S. churches to deepen their ties to Cuban churches.

Family visits and remittances, assisting a growing private sector, expanding cultural and religious contacts, helping Cubans connect to the outside world—if the United States is interested in helping ordinary Cubans and promoting democratic values, these are concrete ways that we can encourage change.

Economic Change in Cuba

Furthermore, even before the opennings set in place by President Obama Cuba was on a trajectory toward economic change. There has been a shift of large numbers of workers to the newly emerging private sector and some market mechanisms have been incorporated. Thousands of Cubans are now renting out their homes on Air BnB and as of December 2015 over 500,000 Cubans were self-employed. Given the increase in tourism that number is now significantly higher and due to increase as small and medium-sized private businesses become legal. The fundamentals of the relationship between Cubans and their government are changing for the first time since the 1959 revolution.

Engagement, even as it intersects with the economic changs underway in Cuba, will not magically transform the nation. What it will do is open contact and dialogue with the whole spectrum of Cuban society – businesses, church, students, medical workers and scientific perfessionals. What they will seek in terms of reform and opening in Cuba will be up to them; we can't and shouldn't dictate the character or the pace of change in Cuba. But there is little doubt that contact and dialogue will encourage and stimulate reformers.

We shouldn't be naïve in our expectations about the political leadership in Cuba. My colleagues on this panel and others will continue to face difficulties and challenges. Cuba will reform on its own terms and in its own time. But the more quickly we move to normalize relations, the more we help create the conditions in which Cuba will update and revise its model in ways that are good for political opening and democracy.

The forms of engagement that President Obama has put into place are constructive. Moving to end the entire embargo would be another positive step for the Cuban people, as well as for the United States. That's a view shared by 72 percent of the American people, according to recent polls, including 53 percentage of Cuban Americans, and over 60 percent of Cuban Americans under 30.

We are at the beginning of a new progress of engagement - a long-term process to build bridges between the American and Cuban people. Over time, engagement will help empower Cuban citizens and open political space in Cuba.

Mr. SMITH. Mr. Thale, thank you very much.

I'd like to begin the questioning first asking Dr. Biscet. Years ago I met Armando Valladares, who had spent numerous years in Cuba prisons. He was tortured horribly. He wrote a book called "Against All Hope," I've read it twice. I actually went with him to the U.N. Human Rights Commission. Frank Calzon has been there many times bearing witness to human rights abuses, including sex trafficking, and I'll never forget reading the book when he described the tortures that were systematic, the Ho Chi Minh poles, the terrible degrading perversions that were imposed upon political prisoners by the guards with the full assent of the Castro brothers for years. And I wonder if you could tell this subcommittee what it was like for you when you were in prison, how were you treated? How much time did you spend in solitary confinement? And if you could just provide us that insight.

It was books like Richard Wumbrand's "Tortured for Christ," which got me into the religious freedom issue back in 1981 when he talked about what Nicholae Ceausescu's secret police, called the Securitate, had done, that it woke up many of us in Congress about what, in that case, Ceausescu was all about.

In the Communist regime of the Soviet Union, Solzhenitsyn laid bare what was going on in the gulags in Siberia. It is important that we know truly what's going on behind those closed doors. If you could provide us with some insight?

[The following was delivered through an interpreter.]

Dr. BISCET. When one wants to know the nature of a society, first visit their prisons. And perhaps that's why the Castro Communist regime doesn't allow anyone to visit; the International Committee of the Red Cross is not allowed in, Amnesty International is not allowed in, Human Rights Watch is not allowed in, because then they would see the perverse nature of that regime. And first you need to remember that what you have in Cuba is a totalitarian Communist regime. You need to remember Stalin, remember Hitler; that's what you have in Cuba.

When many were making a profound critique of torture taking place in the Naval Station Guantanamo Bay prison camp with the terrorists, Fidel Castro at the same time was torturing in Cuba. One of the tortures that they used to commit was to hang people from the roof, from the ceiling with handcuffs with their legs dangling in the air for 10 to 24 hours. Another one was where they handcuffed individuals with their hands behind their back, and also handcuffing their feet in a reverse fetal position and leaving them several hours in their cell in that prone position. Another one is that they used the electric shock gun as a tool of persuasion for those who protest or complain. Another punishment that I saw was to be closed off in a punishment cell sometimes completely closed off, sometimes not, but with people sick with active tuberculosis. Another thing that I saw and suffered were being placed in small cells with people with HIV, but also with people who are mentally ill, and in that process people becoming infected with the virus. In another case they placed me in a very small cell with people who were mentally ill, taking away their psychotropic medication so they would be in a state of delirium so they would attack me. Also, the political police use common political prisoners to force dissenters to cease and desist from their thinking by inciting to beat them. On three occasions, three inmates tried to murder me sent by officials of the prison. And this is how they with these inhuman practices seek to drive mad those who are there innocently. On one occasion, I was kept 5 months in a dark punishment cell. I only received water once a day, and it was at the same spot where one would defecate. In this cell, on one occasion I was without the ability to speak to another human being for 1 month. In broad strokes, those are the tortures applied or carried out in the prisons.

We know that the Castros use the prisons and the common prisoners to try to break the freedom spirit of the Cuban people. In my last years in prison, my last 10 to 12 days, I was just eating bread and water because I feared that the political police would have me murdered. And they not only torture the person who dissents, but also their families. Families, when they go to make their visits, are searched and harassed as if they were criminals. And food and nutrients or vitamins that are taken there are also searched and often damaged in ways that negatively affect the health of the prisoner. And they also use the suspension of family visits as a way to impact not only the family, but also the prisoner. And the most barbaric thing I've seen, also, is the use of medicine as an instrument of torture where patients who are sick are denied medical assistance, and then have died.

Mr. SMITH. As we said, I do have a lot of questions. I'll ask one, yield to my good friend, Albio, and then come back to some of those questions. But let me just thank you for giving us that terrible insight as to what you have endured.

I have tried to get to Cuba for 20 years and have been denied a visa each and every time. Most recently, I met with Jose Cabanas, the Ambassador of Cuba to the United States. He made it clear that if I were to go, I'd have to agree to certain parameters in terms of who I could meet with. And I'm wondering, Mr. Thale, last time you were here in February 2015 testifying, I asked you if you had in your many visits, and I think you said 36 so far, or approximately, whether or not you visited any dissidents in prison, and I'm wondering have you done that, one. And, secondly, did you raise the case with your Cuban interlocutors the case of Dr. Oscar Biscet while you were in Cuba?

Mr. THALE. I have not visited a prison on my trips. I have visited——

Mr. SMITH. Have you requested to do so?

Mr. THALE. No, and I'd be happy to do that, as a matter of fact. In Cuba and in many countries prison systems are terrible places and need to be reformed, and I'd be happy to make that request. And I know there's been discussion about the ICRC visit, so think that's perfectly legitimate.

I have not raised Dr. Biscet's case. I have raised a number of cases, of individual cases as well as general human rights cases with Cuba authorities——

Mr. SMITH. But no specific dissidents, or no dissidents by name?

Mr. THALE. I have named—no, I've named a number of individual cases over the years, including the 75 who were arrested in 2003. I raised that personally with the Cuban Foreign Minister, so

I've raised a range of those cases. I obviously raised the Alan Gross case, as well.

Mr. SMITH. Just so I know, was there any reason why you didn't raise Dr. Biscet? There was a campaign that Albio Sires, Ileana Ros-Lehtinen, Lincoln Diaz-Balart, Mario Diaz-Balart, and I, and many others to have Dr. Biscet named as a Nobel Peace Prize Laureate. I know he was under review for that. It was a global effort. We certainly in Congress had a bipartisan effort to do so. His prominence and his gravitas, his courage, I don't know how he survived all of the cruelty that was imposed upon him. I have no idea. Faith, I'm not sure how he could have survived it, and to be here speaking so eloquently and in such calm tones when he has been so maltreated by a dictatorship. I would have hoped you would have raised his case.

Maybe you could help me get that visa, because I want to go to the prisons. I have been asking—just let me say parenthetically and I, again, will yield to Dr. Biscet. I've been in Chinese gulags, Beijing Prison Number One, when Xanana Gusmao of East Timor was in a Jakarta prison. Jakarta, the Indonesians allowed me into that prison. Along with Frank Wolf, we got in during the worst days of the Soviet Union into Perm Camp 35 which is where Sharansky was held and many other political prisoners. All of those dictatorships allowed us in into the prisons, and we can't get into the prisons of Castro's Cuba. It is very telling. Albio.

Mr. SIRES. Thank you, Mr. Chairman. Dr. Biscet, thank you very much.

You know, Mr. Thale, I came here when I was 11 years old, 1962, and I have been dealing with the Cuban community where I live ever since. I represent the second largest concentration of Cuban-Americans outside of Miami. And I get that 55 years or 57 years without any kind of talking. It's a long time, but my biggest complaint is that we have given away pressure points where we could have drawn concessions from the Cuban Government. At a time when Venezuela can no longer provide the kind of assistance that it provided before, at a time when Russia can't actually do anything for Cuba, Cuba seems to be on its own, and we seem to be throwing them a lifesaver, in terms of getting concessions from them. This government is not going to give any concessions until some pressure is put on them. And the President can go to Cuba, the Pope can go to Cuba, two Popes can go to Cuba and nothing changes. So to me, you know, this picture that you paint of all these changes, I disagree with you. I don't think it's that great of a change.

People go to Cuba, they tell you who you can meet with. Have you met with dissidents? Do you get a chance to meet with any dissidents you want? Because I know that Members come, you know, first thing they tell the Members when they go to Cuba is this is the group of people you can't meet with.

I'm not finished yet. In terms of the economy, 85 percent of the economy in Cuba is controlled by the government. When they talk about economic growth for the people of Cuba, we're not talking about the people of Cuba. Maybe they own an ice cream parlor, maybe they sell hot dogs, maybe they sell hamburgers, but still you have companies that go to Cuba and they have to ask the government for the workers. And the government tells you what to pay, and then they in turn pay peanuts to the workers of Cuba. So how are the Cuban people going to benefit?

My complaint is we just don't insist on concessions from this government. And, you know, I don't know, I've made it clear to the President. I'm not telling you anything that I haven't told the White House, or I have said at the committee. But, you know, negotiations are a two-way street. Now they want Bank of Cuba, they want Cuba to buy—they don't—they can't buy anything. They're one of the biggest debtor nations in the world, so how are they going to buy anything? They're going to run billions of dollars of debt and then they're going to expect people to forgive the money. So I know we have to start someplace, but my biggest problem is we started and we didn't get any real concessions.

And in terms of JoAnne Chesimard, I'm constantly meeting with the State Troopers in New Jersey. I was the Speaker of the House in New Jersey for 4 years. We went down Florida when they put the $1 million bounty on JoAnne Chesimard, and we had a press conference. Now it's $2 million. And now they're talking about exchanging prisoners, Montes for JoAnne Chesimard. There's no reason we should give up a spy because you have a person who shot somebody point blank on the New Jersey Turnpike and ran to Cuba, and has been living there as if she was a hero.

So, I get your position, I understand your job. You get your orders, but what I have said to you I have told the people at the White House. I've been here 10 years and I've been firm on my position. You want something for Cuba, give me something in return. Stop the abuses. Just listen to some of the abuses. Why must we always give in?

And as far as all the—I get this—people tell me all the time oh, we now have a better relation with everybody else because now—there's not one country that has spoken up about the abuses of human rights in Cuba for 18 months. I hear Argentina talking about the abuses in Venezuela, but I don't hear anybody talking about the abuses in Cuba. So that argument to me is bogus because they don't speak, they're afraid of the Cuban Government. They're afraid that they may foment the college studies and the universities in their country against the government if they speak up. So there you have it; tell me what you think.

Mr. THALE. Well, thank you, Congressman Sires. Respectfully, obviously, we do see the situation differently. I've had family that lived in Cuba at one time or another, but I'm not Cuban-American, and my family members were passing through. My family is Irish, and they feel—through three generations feel personal and incredibly powerful stories about the British and their attitude toward the Irish. And I understand those kind of strong personal feelings. So I understand, and I think we've heard stories here that are very real, and very powerful. I understand the importance of that.

My view is that the decision to normalize relations was made because it was—I think because it was in the U.S. national interest to do so. I think it did help with our relationship with other partners in the hemisphere, particularly with Colombia. I think it does help with some of our business interests, and I think it's fundamentally clear that what we have done over the last 57 years, which is to say no concessions, no nothing until you change or collapse hasn't worked, so I think we need a new approach. I don't think that the Obama administration came in, and I know we'll dispute about this, but came in saying we're going to make concessions. I think the Obama administration came in saying we are going to take a new approach that's in our interest, and that we believe over time will lead to change in your society. I don't think it came in saying the changes will be A, B, C, and D in exactly this order, and we're going to tell you what to do, but I think it came in believing that engagement and ending hostility is more likely to generate greater flexibility and more people inside Cuba and inside Cuban society who want to push for change internally and on their own terms. And I think we're beginning to see that. I don't think it's easy. I don't think any of this process is magical, but I don't— but I do think that over time it's far more likely to make a difference.

Mr. SIRES. I want the best for Cuba. I just think we have different ways from my experience, my life experience of how to approach and deal with the Cuban Government. I'll just give you an example that just happened to me. My aunt came from Cuba not too long ago. She went back to see her daughter. I asked her to get me a copy of my birth certificate. She went to the Municipal Building, they denied my birth certificate because they said I was a terrorist. So like anything in Cuba, they gave $20 to somebody, I have four copies in my house today. I can tell you other things that has happened to families of mine because they're related to me, how they lost their job, how they pressure the family. And people that were educated on the island, and educated in Russia, once they found out they were my cousins, they became persona non grata. So, you know, I do have emotional ties to Cuba, but my biggest problem is look, let's negotiate, let's negotiate.

And this business that the Cuban people are improving the economy when 85 percent of the economy is run by the government, and if you don't work for the government you can't get a job, which is what happened to my cousin. He was an engineer; he lost his job. And where do you go; you're an engineer in Cuba and you don't work for the government? You become a taxi driver.

Mr. THALE. The emerging private sector in Cuba does probably include between 25 and 30 percent of the workforce. Within that, there's a small set of people who are making real money. I think there's very little question about that. And then there actually is— we're beginning to see for the first time in 55 years people working in the private sector for others. Right now, those people are probably making more than they'd make in the state sector; although, down the road we'll have to see what happens there. But there is an emerging private sector. It is not the——

Mr. SIRES. It's a small group of people that are benefitting from the tourists, but it's not the island or the workforce of the island. That's still controlled by the government.

Mr. THALE. So the government workforce is probably 70 percent, 75 percent. It's smaller than it was, but it's clearly an overwhelmingly majority; that's true. All I'm saying is that we are seeing the beginnings of a small private sector emerging, and within that we're seeing some workers and some owners.

Mr. SIRES. Mr. Thale, quite frankly, a lot of that force, a lot of those people were there before the engagement. Okay? A lot of these people that were selling and trading, and everything else, it was there before we did this engagement with them, so there was already a small amount of people trading back and forth within the country. You can only repress an economy so much. The Cuban people tend to be pretty good at making a buck, whether it's here or there. Thank you.

Mr. SMITH. Thank you, Mr. Sires.

I'll ask a question or two, then yield to my friend. And then I have some final questions after that.

The Washington Post has been probably the most outspoken in its editorial pages; one of the editorials was ''Failure in Cuba.'' They've had a series of important statements to be made. They've pointed out that the economic lifeline to Cuba when the Soviet Union diminished, then Russia in terms of their ability to provide economic assistance to Cuba; Venezuela, with the decline of oil prices they lost their capability. Now they're really in dire straits and cannot funnel money to Havana. And then the U.S. stepped in right at the precise time to keep the dictatorship afloat.

The Washington Post, one of their editorials, on January 31 said, ''Mr. Obama continues to offer the Castro regime unilateral concessions requiring nothing in return. Since the United States has placed no human rights conditions on the opening, the Castro regime continues to systematically engage in arbitrary detention of dissidents and others who speak up for democracy. In fact, detentions have spiked in recent months. The state continues to monopolize radio, television, and newspapers.''

In another just published editorial, this by Jackson Diehl, deputy editorial page editor, he writes and he does profile Dr. Biscet. He says that, ''Obama's policy has had the effect of stranding the most American pro-democracy people in Cuba, the activists who have spent their lives fighting the system at enormous personal cost. While the regime collects U.S. cooperation in dollars, repression of the opposition has sharply increased. According to the Cuban Commission for Human Rights, there were 6,075 political arrests during the first 5 months of this year, 2016, the highest number in decades.'' If that isn't a clear suggestion of a failed policy, wait, and wait for what, as things go from bad to worse, as more people are being rounded up, as catch and release becomes the modus operandi for the Castro brothers. So I think we need to put this in perspective.

I was for the Apartheid sanctions against South Africa, the sanctions against Russia most recently, the sanctions against China when they were in place. Unfortunately, they've been lifted, and we have seen a diminution of human rights respect under Xi Jinping's regime in the People's Republic of China. We put sanctions on in order to say we're not kidding, conditions are about human rights, and about the great people like Dr. Biscet and others who are suffering unspeakable cruelty because they want freedom and democracy.

I would ask a question, how many people—and maybe, Ms. Werlau, you might have this answer, one of you might. How many people has the Castro regime tortured over these many decades?

How many people have they killed because of their political positions? It seems to me the number is so high, and I've seen estimates, but I would appreciate your thoughts, that the Castro brothers ought to be referred from the Security Council to the International Criminal Court, the ICC, the tribunal for crimes against humanity. We are talking about large numbers of people over the course of many decades, systematic repression and, of course, a systematic murdering of people who don't agree with the regime. Your thoughts? And, again, if anyone has any insights as to how many people. Ms. Werlau?

Ms. WERLAU. I don't think anybody can answer how many people because we simply don't know. But I just want to point out that the Stasi files that were recovered point to around 60,000 political prisoners, I forgot, I think in the early 1970s or late 1960s. There are just no statistics.

But I do want to say something that comes to mind. We do know how many the Pinochet dictatorship killed in its 15-year life, and that's 3,187 is the total of disappeared and killed by the Pinochet regime. And I never heard any human rights organization argue that we must engage the Pinochet regime on its own terms, that we must somehow convince them, by giving people cell phones or whatever, that they need to change. The fact of the matter is, the Chilean society was never totalitarian, and yet the whole community, the whole worldwide community, condemned dictatorship in Chile. And that's what's been missing, a multilateral approach to say we're not going to engage an illegitimate criminal regime on its terms. We're going to demand conditions.

What has failed is that government. Engagement has been tried by European countries, by Canada, by Latin America for decades; we traded, invested, supported, given credibility, given assistance to Cuba, you name it, and nothing has worked. What we need to do is to try to get a multilateral approach to understand that that is the nature of that regime, that we must set conditions to engage it.

[The following was delivered through an interpreter.]

Ms. AVILA LEON. I was surprised to hear the defense of the regime by the gentleman on my left. The rental houses provided by the regime have been used as a reward for torture, for assaults. This is similar to what happened with the opening of agricultural and other properties, that it was done for a show externally, but it was being provided to those with privileges in the regime, with those that are well connected. It's not something that helps the Cuban people.

And if you want a more clearer demonstration of the failure of this policy, is what happened within hours of President Obama's arrival in Havana, which was the repression and violence visited upon the Ladies in White in Todos Marchamos.

Sole proprietors are getting most of the money. They're there to control tourists, they are getting their remittances, but I can provide firsthand evidence. My son, who was 18½ years a member of the Cuban Armed Forces for not tying me down and declaring me insane was fired from the Armed Forces, and is unable to get work now.

I believe that the gentleman who was testifying to my left, what he's reporting on is the regime's propaganda campaign. It's what he's observing. The investors and the tourists are a smokescreen that do not demonstrate the profound poverty that the Cuban people are submerged in, the cruel poverty, which really does descend to the level of slavery in terms of the little payment that is provided for those who work in the government sector. And I invite those who have this view, if they come to Cuba to walk with me, and I can show them the real Cuba.

[The following was delivered through an interpreter.]

Dr. BISCET. I think we need to remember people, we who are present here, that when I said that this regime is Hitler and Stalin-like, it is Hitler and Stalin-like. The number of dead may not be the same, but there is a machinery of death that operates as that of Hitler and Stalin. They arrived in power January 1, 1959. Raul Castro engaged in the first mass execution with a mass grave in the first month of the revolution; 900 people in the first month were executed, 500 of them for thinking differently. They did not pertain to the previous regime. The death penalty exists to terrorize the population and to control it.

Prior to the revolution between 1902 and 1950, there was no practical death penalty in practice in Cuba. There was a regulation that if someone in the military was a traitor to their country with a foreign power, they could be executed, but beyond that it didn't exist on paper, and it wasn't applied in practice.

This dictatorship has engaged in mass executions, mass jailings, mass confiscations of properties to impose state terror, and to use the state terror to control the Cuban people through fear. So it really is state terrorism, and there is a Cold War continuing in our country, but it is against our own people. And these days because that terror has been so effective, it doesn't have to be a mass terror, it's a selective terror against all who raise their voice, all who associate freely or assemble freely. They can be targeted.

The last three young men to be executed in Cuba in 2003, young Afro-Cuban men, were executed with the purpose of terrorizing the Cuban population, especially the Afro-Cuban population. Since then there have been no more executions, but the death penalty remains on the books. Raul Castro has said that if they need to do what they did in 2003, they will do it again. And please have that present.

Ms. BASS. Okay, we're going to be called for votes in just a second. Okay, I just wanted to say a couple of things. Number one, I do hope that I see the day in the United States that we get rid of the death penalty, as well.

I just wanted to correct a couple of things, or at least give my viewpoint, anyway, of President Obama's visit. I was there with the President, and I thought it was frankly extremely remarkable that the President of the United States spoke to the Cuban people and was quite openly critical of Cuba. He had a meeting with dissidents, and the people that he met with were chosen by the U.S. Embassy, they were not chosen by the Cuban Government. I think, frankly, that that was a very remarkable thing, and I could only imagine a head of state coming to the United States and meeting with a group of Black Lives Matter or other people here who have issues, or raise issues in the United States and say that Raul Castro wants to come and visit San Quentin, or wants to raise questions about what it happening in this country, raising questions about the African-American population in the United States, why so many people have been killed by police officers, why the unemployment rate is so high, why the education rate is low, why we have systemic discrimination in the United States.

So I think that, to me, 50 years of one policy that didn't work, I understand the definition of insanity is to keep going the same thing and then expect different results. To me, it makes sense that we have a new policy and it is certainly my understanding when the Obama administration has been in negotiations with the Cuban Government, that they have consistently raised human rights, human rights violations. And it's my understanding that when we engage in negotiations with many other countries, that that is also what we do. We don't leave that off the table.

With that, I'm going to go vote. Thank you. I'll yield back to the chair.

Mr. SMITH. Thank you very much. Dr. Biscet, you wanted to finish your comment?

[The following was delivered through an interpreter.]

Dr. BISCET. I think it's important because we just brought up the issue of race, and I think it's important that we talk about the issue of race in Cuba.

In the U.S., these difficulties can be resolved in the court of law where the judiciary is independent, but in Cuba the courts are subject to the arbitrary whims of the executive.

The Afro-Cuban population in Cuba is one that's most discriminated against, but that's not the greatest issue confronting Cuba. The greatest issue is the political and ideological apartheid that exists in the country where all persons who think or speak differently are discriminated and looked down upon by the Cuban regime.

In Cuba there's no right to vote, there's no right to free elections. The elemental human rights that are defended so much here in the United States are what is lacking, or what are lacking in Cuba. The history of the United States and the people of the United States is a beautiful story of integration. When you fought for your independence from Great Britain, there were Cubans on the island who sent assistance to help you in your struggle. There were poor families in Cuba that although they had very few resources gave what little they had to assist in the independence of the United States. And we're also very proud that the American people took a part in the independence of Cuba. And when the Joint Resolution of 1898 was done, it guaranteed the independence and freedom of the Cuban nation. Four years in 1902, thanks to this Joint Resolution to this document, the Cubans had their freedom and their independence. And it was signed here in this place by this Congress, and signed by President McKinley.

And we also have to be proud of another law that exists today, which is the law of freedom and solidarity, otherwise known as the Helms-Burton Law which guarantees a democratic Cuba. And that document has within it that law, that to have diplomatic relations that the regime or the government that you're dealing with has to be undergoing a transition to democracy, or that it be a democratic government. Nevertheless, this law has been violated by the administration that's actually in power. Our people are still living under this modern slavery which is communism and socialism.

Many years ago, your country had a Civil War because part of the country wanted to maintain part of the population in slavery, and that violated the U.S. Constitution; principally, those basic human rights found in the Bill of Rights. We have our own Rights Charter like that of the Bill of Rights in our Constitution of 1940. And for that reason I ask Representative Starling to reflect on this, that all those rights found in the 1940 Constitution have been abrogated in a de facto manner. And that's what we want, we want to have the same rights you have. And please take a look at the conditions on the ground before you start giving additional concessions.

I want to show you something beautiful. The first thing that free Cuban people did when they got their independence was to have a referendum of what statue they would place in Havana. The Cubans voted for our Apostle Jose Marti, and while they waited for the building of the statue of Jose Marti, they inaugurated another statue remembering America; and that is the Statue of Liberty in the Central Park of Cuba, which is the most famous park in Cuba. That's what the United States represents to Cuba, freedom.

Mr. SMITH. Dr. Biscet, we're out of time for 14 votes that have just occurred on the House floor. I want to thank you, and thank all of you for your testimony. I wish this could go longer, but it is on zero, and I will miss an important vote on Iran. So I want to thank you.

I have some additional questions on trafficking. Yesterday, the administration gave an upgrade again for the second year in a row to Cuba. I wrote that law on trafficking. I think it was a horrific decision politically motivated, and my hope is that they will revisit it even before next year because it was a mistake to give a passing grade to a country where sex and labor trafficking flourishes.

The hearing is adjourned, and again I thank you. I do have to run.

[Whereupon, at 5:24 p.m., the subcommittee was adjourned.]

A P P E N D I X

Material Submitted for the Record

SUBCOMMITTEE HEARING NOTICE
COMMITTEE ON FOREIGN AFFAIRS
U.S. HOUSE OF REPRESENTATIVES
WASHINGTON, DC 20515-6128

Subcommittee on Africa, Global Health, Global Human Rights, and International Organizations
Christopher H. Smith (R-NJ), Chairman

July 13, 2016

TO: MEMBERS OF THE COMMITTEE ON FOREIGN AFFAIRS

You are respectfully requested to attend an OPEN hearing of the Committee on Foreign Affairs, to be held by the Subcommittee on Africa, Global Health, Global Human Rights, and International Organizations in Room 2172 of the Rayburn House Office Building (and available live on the Committee website at http://www.ForeignAffairs.house.gov):

DATE: Wednesday, July 13, 2016

TIME: 2:00 p.m.

SUBJECT: The Castro Regime's Ongoing Violations of Civil and Political Rights

WITNESSES: Oscar Elias Biscet, M.D.
President
Lawton Foundation for Human Rights
(Former Cuban political prisoner)

Ms. Sirley Avila Leon
Democracy Advocate

Ms. Maria Werlau
President
Free Society Project

Mr. Geoff Thale
Program Director
Washington Office on Latin America

By Direction of the Chairman

The Committee on Foreign Affairs seeks to make its facilities accessible to persons with disabilities. If you are in need of special accommodations, please call 202/225-5021 at least four business days in advance of the event, whenever practicable. Questions with regard to special accommodations in general (including availability of Committee materials in alternative formats and assistive listening devices) may be directed to the Committee.

COMMITTEE ON FOREIGN AFFAIRS

MINUTES OF SUBCOMMITTEE ON _Africa, Global Health, Global Human Rights, and International Organizations_ HEARING

Day_____*Wednesday*_____Date_____ *July 13, 2016*_____Room_*2172 Rayburn HOB*_

Starting Time___*3:36 p.m.*___Ending Time___*5:24 p.m.*___

Recesses | *0* | (___to_*0*_) (___to___) (___to___) (___to___) (___to___) (___to___)

Presiding Member(s)

Rep. Chris Smith

Check all of the following that apply:

Open Session ☑
Executive (closed) Session ☐
Televised ☑

Electronically Recorded (taped) ☑
Stenographic Record ☑

TITLE OF HEARING:

The Castro Regime's Ongoing Violations of Civil and Political Rights

SUBCOMMITTEE MEMBERS PRESENT:

Rep. Karen Bass

NON-SUBCOMMITTEE MEMBERS PRESENT: *(Mark with an * if they are not members of full committee.)*

Rep. Albio Sires

HEARING WITNESSES: Same as meeting notice attached? Yes ☑ No ☐
(If "no", please list below and include title, agency, department, or organization.)

STATEMENTS FOR THE RECORD: *(List any statements submitted for the record.)*

List of political prisoners in Cuba, submitted by Rep. Chris Smith
Question for the record for Mr. Geoff Thale from Rep. Chris Smith

TIME SCHEDULED TO RECONVENE _____
or
TIME ADJOURNED ___*5:24 p.m.*___

_____
Subcommittee Staff Associate

MATERIAL SUBMITTED FOR THE RECORD BY THE HONORABLE CHRISTOPHER H. SMITH, A REPRESENTATIVE IN CONGRESS FROM THE STATE OF NEW JERSEY, AND CHAIRMAN, SUBCOMMITTEE ON AFRICA, GLOBAL HEALTH, GLOBAL HUMAN RIGHTS, AND INTERNATIONAL ORGANIZATIONS

Preliminary list of political prisoners in Cuba
Cuban Democratic Directorate
March 21, 2016

1. Yasiel Espino Aceval/ Condemnded 4 years/ Ariza Prison
2. Alexander Palacio Reyes/ Cerámica Roja Prison
3. Alexis Serrano Avila/Condemned 3 years prison
4. Andrés Fidel Alfonso Rodríguez/ Melena Sur prison
5. Ernesto Borges Pérez/ Combinado del Este prison
6. Carlos Amaury Calderin Roca/ Valle Grande prison
7. Maria del Carmen Cala Aguilera/Pendiente/Provincial Women's Prison Holguín Province
8. Enrique Bartolomé Cambria Diaz/ Kilo 8 prison
9. Misael Canet Velázquez/ Kilo 8 prison
10. Santiago Cisneros Castellanos/Pendiente/ Aguadores prison
11. Leonardo Cobas Pérez/ Moscú prison
12. Felipe Martin Companione/ Cerámica Roja prison Condemned to 8 years in prison
13. Orlando Contreras Aguiar/ Aguacate prison
14. Yeri Curbelo Aguilera/Condemned 3 years prison/Guantanamo Prison
15. Pedro de la Caridad Alvarez Pedroso
16. Jordys Manuel Dosil/Condemned 3 years prison
17. Carlos Manuel Figueroa Álvarez/ Combinado del Este Prison/ Condemned to 6 years prison
18. David Fernández Cardoso/ Bungo Ocho Prison
19. José Daniel Gonzalez Fumero/ Nieves Morejón Prison
20. Ricardo González Sendiña/condemned 6 years/Combinado del Este
21. Ariel González Sendiña/ condemned 6 years/Combinado del Este
22. Eglis Heredia Rodríguez/ Boniato Prison
23. Mario Alberto Hernández Leiva/Melena del Sur prison/Condemned to 3 years prison
24. Geovanys Izaguirre Hernández/ Aguadores Prison
25. Rolando Erismelio Jaco García/ Cerámica Roja Prison
26. Javier Jouz Varona/Social Dangerousness prison / Condemned to 3 years prison
27. Isain López Luna/ Valle Grande Prison
28. Noel López Gonzalez/ Condemned 12 years prison
29. Michael Mediaceja Ramos/Condemned 6 months / Guanajay prison
30. Osmaní Mendosa Ferrior/ Las Mangas prison
31. Mario Morera Jardines/Condemned to 3 years prison / Guamajal prison
32. Ernesto Ortega Sarduy/ Valle Grande prison
33. Ricardo Pelier Frómeta/Condemned to 3 years jail / Combinado de Guantanamo prison
34. Fernando Isael Peña Tamayo/ Condemned to 5 years / El Típico prison
35. Silverio Portal Contreras/ Campamento Ochimán prison
36. Humberto Eladio Real Suarez
37. René Rouco Machin/ Melena del Sur prison
38. Laudelino Rodriguez Mendoza/ Granjita prison, Santiago de Cuba
39. Leoncio Rodriguez Poncio/Condemned to 42 years and has served 28 years in prison/Guantanamo Prison
40. Alfredo Luis Limonte Rodriguez/Condemned 4 years / Ariza Prison
41. Elieski Roque Chongo/ Condemned 5 years / Ariza Prison

42. Alexander Alan Rodríguez/Sentence Pending / Valle Grande Prison
43. Reinier Rodríguez Mendoza/ Condemned to 2 years of prison / San José Prison
44. Mario Ronaide Figueroa Reyes/ Condemned to 3 years prison / Prision 1580
45. Yoelkis Rozábal Flores/Condemned to 4 years / Combinado de Guantánamo prison
46. Daniel Santovenia Fernandez
47. Emilio Serrano Rodriguez/Valle Grande Prison
48. Armando Sosa Fortuny/Camaguey Prison
49. Liusban John Ultra/Condemned to 7 years/Jailed in the Province of Las Tunas/La Granjita Prison
50. Armado Verdecía Díaz/Condemned to 5 years of prison/Malverde Prison

Sources:

Directorio Democrático Cubano
Andry Frometa Cuenca, former political prisoner
Yordan Marrero, Partido Democráta Cristiano de Camagüey
Librado Linares Garcia, General Secretary of the Movimiento Cubano Reflexión
Unión Patriótica de Cuba (UNPACU)

Question for the Record Submitted to
Mr. Geoff Thale
by Representative Chris Smith
House Committee on Foreign Affairs
Subcommittee on Africa, Global Health, Global Human Rights, and International
Organizations
July 13, 2016

Question:

The Department of State's 2014 Trafficking in Person's Report had designated Cuba as a Tier 3 country of concern – the worst designation for trafficking – and Cuba had been listed as a Tier 3 country of concern ever year it has appeared in the report. That is, until the 2015 report, when Cuba was upgraded to Tier 2 Watch List. While still noting in the commentary that the penal code does not criminalize all forms of trafficking, in particular force labor and sex trafficking of children ages 16 and 17, Cuba nevertheless received an upgrade. Do you think this upgrade was justified, or was it motivated by political calculations, a reward to the regime by the Obama administration for steps taken to normalize relations?

Answer:

[No response received at time of printing]